Weather

Le temps

ler toh

Illustrated by Clare Beaton

Illustré par Clare Beaton

b small publishing

rain

la pluie

lah plwee

sun

le soleil

ler sol*ay*

fog

le brouillard

ler brwee-*yar*

snow

la neige

lah neh-jsh

ice

la glace

lah gla'ss

wind

le vent

ler voh

cloud

le nuage

ler nooah-jsh

thunder

le tonnerre

ler ton*air*

lightning

les éclairs

lezeh-*clair*

storm

l'orage

lor*ah*–jsh

rainbow

l'arc-en-ciel

larkon-see-ell

A simple guide to pronouncing the French words

- Read this guide as naturally as possible, as if it were standard British English.
- Put stress on the letters in *italics* e.g. ler ton*air*
- Don't roll the r at the end of the word, e.g. in the French word le (the): ler.

Le temps	ler toh	**Weather**
la pluie	la plwee	**rain**
le soleil	le sol*ay*	**sun**
le brouillard	ler brwee-*yar*	**fog**
la neige	lah neh-jsh	**snow**
la glace	lah gla'ss	**ice**
le vent	ler voh	**wind**
le nuage	ler noo*ah*-jsh	**cloud**
le tonnerre	ler ton*air*	**thunder**
les éclairs	lezeh-*clair*	**lightning**
l'orage	lor*ah*-jsh	**storm**
l'arc-en-ciel	larkon-see-*ell*	**rainbow**

Published by b small publishing
The Book Shed, 36 Leyborne Park, Kew, Richmond, Surrey, TW9 3HA, UK
www.bsmall.co.uk
© b small publishing, 2001 and 2008 (new cover)
1 2 3
All rights reserved.
Printed in China by WKT Company Ltd.
ISBN-13: 978-1-874735-89-2 (UK paperback)
Cataloguing-in-Publication Data:
A catalogue record for this book is available from the British Library